# *Drawings and Collages*

SATISH GUJRAL

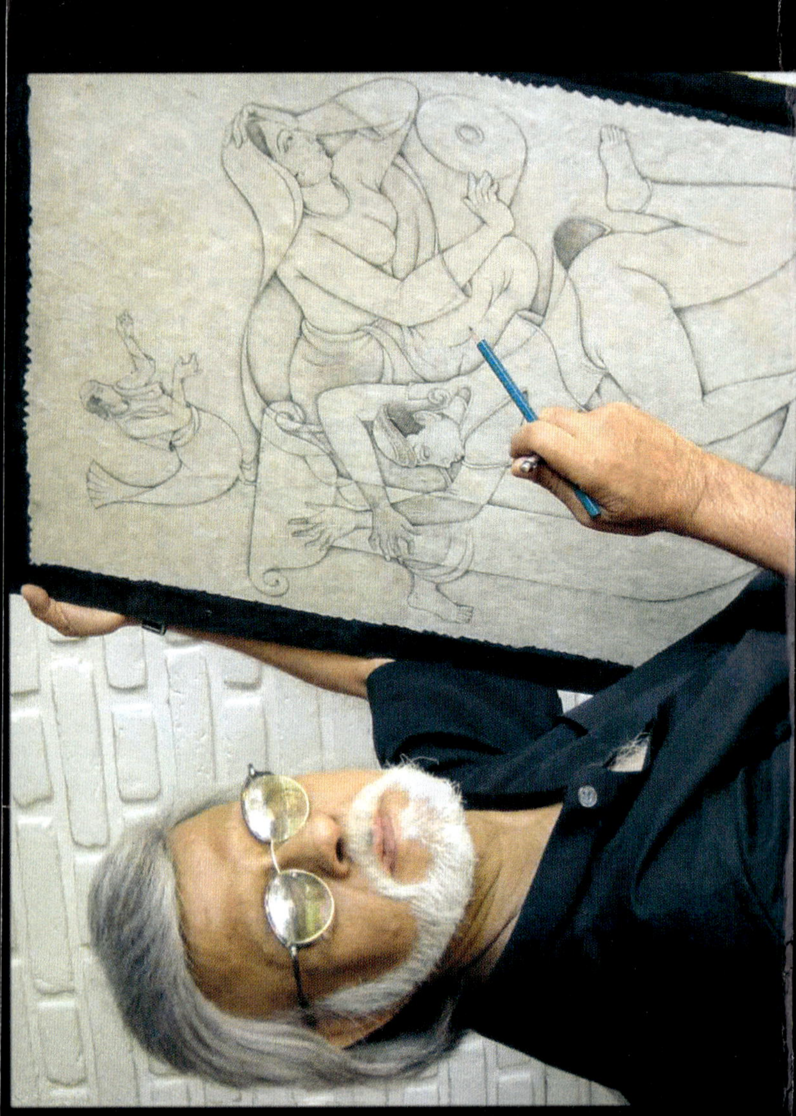

# SATISH GUJRAL

## *Drawings and Collages*

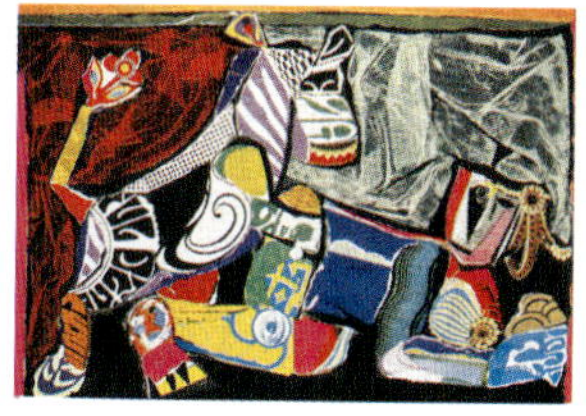

Gayatri Sinha

**Lustre Press**

**Roli Books**

'It has been said that I am obsessed with showing motion. Motion is in a way an alternate to sound, because stillness and silence are one.'

If an artist is both a poet and a craftsman, then Satish Gujral has been honing his skills for over six decades.

Gujral's choice of art as a career was borne of circumstances that were fortuitous and unfortunate. Years of illness forced him to spend protracted periods, from the age of ten to eighteen, as an invalid. Gujral makes light of those childhood exercises, yet it was the doodling that he indulged in, in his sick bed that persuaded his father to foster the boy's graphic capability. As a last-ditch effort at an education, however unconventional, Satish Gujral was admitted as a boarder at the age of thirteen to the Mayo School of Art, Lahore. It was there that he studied drawing, along with stone and woodcarving, metal smithery, and clay moulding, with a distinct emphasis on artisanal values. It is this multiplicity of training that is reflected virtually everywhere in his highly versatile career.

When Gujral graduated from the Mayo School, the careers open to him included painting cinema hoardings, graphic art with an advertising agency, or enlisting as a civil engineer. Instead he continued his studies at the J.J. School of Art in Bombay, where the prime influence on him was another Punjabi artist, Pran Nath Mago, and the folk inspirations of Jamini Roy. Gujral was already familiar with the leading figures of the Lahore art scene – the modernist Roop Krishna who championed the prevailing Bloomsbury fashion in England, and Abdur Rehman Chughtai, who favoured a revival of Persian and provincial Mughal-style drawing. In his second year of college, however, Gujral fell prey

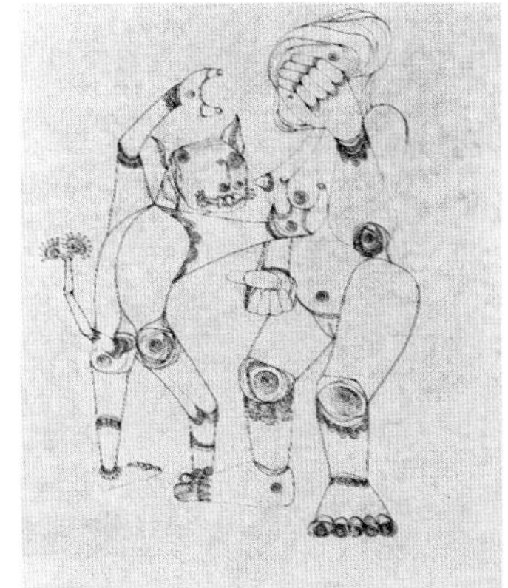

Untitled, 30" ht., drawing

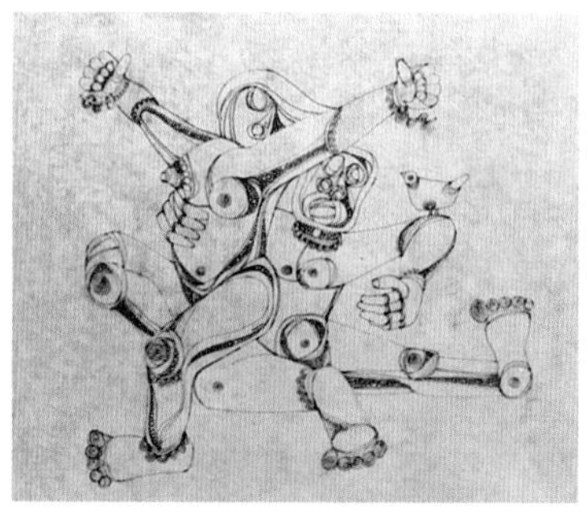

Untitled, 24" x 30", drawing

again to his childhood afflictions. Forced by ill health to return to his home town, Jhelum, he got caught up in the violent partition of Punjab.

Satish Gujral, who helped his father ferry refugees into India, had a stark, indelible view of the trauma of mass displacement and violence. Recuperating from his debilitating condition in Shimla, in the aftermath of the violence, he began to create the works known as his Partition series. Like the paintings of this series which continued intermittently from 1948 to 1960, his drawings too had a powerful expressionistic line – violent gestures and expressions contorted by the extremity of terrible conflict. Prominent among these were the drawings *Mourning en Masse* (1947-48), and *Snare of Memory* (1954). In *Snare of Memory* the clash of metal was evoked by metallic hues and dagger-like forms that thrust and pierced the surroundings. In *Mourning en Masse* the veiled figures of women, heavy and turgid with sorrow, appeared to sway to the rhythm of their own wailing. In a third drawing of the series – *Days of Glory* (1952), refugees huddled together for comfort in their position of reduced penury. Common to all these works were the curvilinear figures, prominently foregrounded in their loss and grief. Strong and rhythmic, this is a line that Gujral has adapted in different materials and textures to produce a body of work, separate and yet interrelated.

Gujral refers to the Partition works as reflecting much more than an externality of subject matter. Rather, they became a medium to express his inner torment, his anguish at the vicissitudes wrought by his own handicap. Reviewing his works in his first solo exhibition organised by Delhi Shilpi Chakra in 1952, the critic Charles Fabri commented that the artist only saw the dark side of life, but life was like a pillar with both bright and dark aspects. Gujral's response was to say that no one could see both sides of the pillar at the same time, and that when he turned around into the stretch of illumination, he would depict that too.

Satish Gujral lived and worked in Mexico, from 1952-54 as the apprentice of the famed Mexican muralist David Alfara Sequiros, under whom Jackson Pollock had worked some years before. The fifties and sixties in India marked the first post-Independence rush to the epicentres of western modernism – Paris and New York. Satish Gujral was an exception in that he went to Mexico, where the graph of the nationalist struggle, and reassertion of ethnicity was closer to the reality of Nehruvian India. Certainly Gujral, even in the early years, was not enamoured of western assertions on Indian soil.

On his return, he executed a mural in Gandhi Bhawan, Punjab University, Chandigarh. This single work signalled the end of his Partition phase. His drawings of the period had a muralesque monumentally in their scope, if not their size. Large animal forms, diminutive humans or figures in energetic sexual play were vigorously executed. The rhythm and energy of these figures was communicated through their prominent hands and feet. It is important to recall that Gujral in his early career was a leftist and was likely to have privileged the qualities of labour and mass energy. It was also in the early 1960s that artists like the Progressive Group decided to categorise drawing as an independent medium.

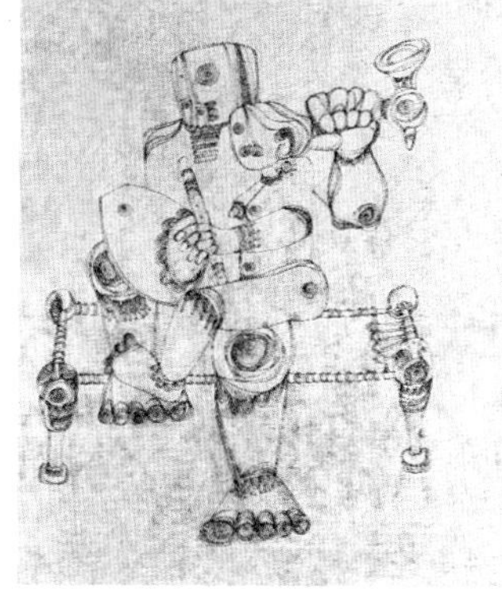

Untitled, 24" x 30", drawing

From this early phase of a tempestuous draughtsmanship, Gujral moved rapidly into the area of paper collage. His collages were based on drawings of the mid 1960s. At the time, no contemporary artist had exploited the possibilities of collage. Gujral chose paper of varied character and density, using opaque printed and transparent matter, torn and arranged in juxtaposition to create suggestions of varied textures.

In a way this heralded the manner in which Gujral has over the years, abandoned one medium to enter another, with a visible sense of freedom and release. The paper collages initiated in 1965-66 had an exuberance and energy that made them distinct in his oeuvre. These collages were done virtually concurrently with his murals, but had a fluidity of line and a quality of abstraction not seen in the use of the more hard-edged ceramic murals.

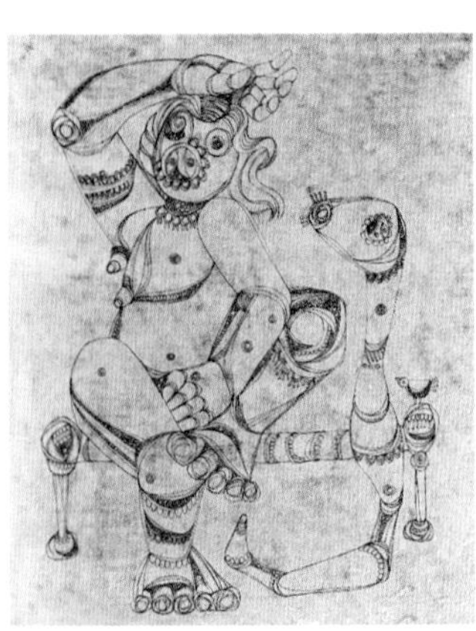
Untitled, 24" x 30", drawing

Using collage's inherent law of chance, Gujral experimented with the fluid possibilities of construction in paper. Collage had been invented by Picasso in the small but watershed work *Still Life with Chair Caning* (1912) in which he had pasted cloth directly on the canvas, incorporating 'low' elements into 'high' art. In the same year Braque went a step further by inventing the paper colle' or pasted paper, setting into process the use of a medium of provocation and possibility. In his paper collages Gujral is actually restrained in his use of materials in that he uses only paper – not even the newsprint that the Cubists used, to bring a provocative political content to their work. However, paper itself is injected with dynamic possibility in its virtual defiance of symmetry and cognitive energy through the unexpected interplay of colour and form.

Within the collages he made a small series titled *Playmates* (1967) in which the dodging energy of childhood, and fluid bend of forms of animals at play, is evident.

Of all the leading Indian contemporaries, Satish Gujral has the most diverse oeuvre, extending from painting to ceramic, collage, sculpture, murals and architecture. The common thread running through this multiple activity is his drawing. 'I start with nature in every phase. After that distortion may be used to look for the latent potential of the form'. In the drawings of the mid '60s and later that coincided with more geometricised abstract forms, the same bird, animal, and human figures of the earlier period were presented in a more reductive form. The metallic sculptures and ceramic murals that came rapidly at this juncture were also reflected in the drawing. 'A drawing is like a deposit. I might sketch on newspapers or even old envelopes – and then finally take from sketches here and there to make a composition. But if an artist does not pass through an evolutionary phase I would doubt his genuineness.'

When Satish Gujral returned to drawing, however, as a full-fledged form in the late 1990s, it was to the inherent calling and grace of the human figure. 'In each period, even if I paint or sculpt, I feel I am drawing. The significance of drawing is that you keep trying to keep your eyes on life. Drawing is the edge of life.'

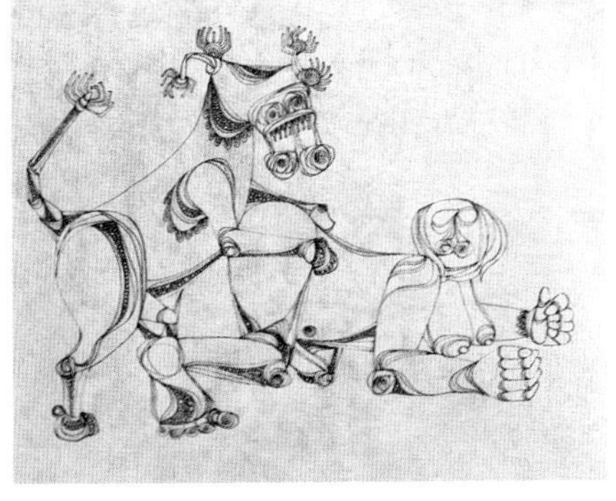
Untitled, 24" x 30", drawing

Gujral particularly admires the drawings of El Greco, the Mexican artist Jose Clemente Orozco, and the Indian artist Shiavax Chavda who painted and drew dancers and musicians, a theme that attracted Gujral in his later phase. Orozco's influence of scenes of everyday life, of human degradation and exaltation, and concern with his own national ethos undoubtedly influenced Gujral in the early years. However, the artist has also continually absorbed from the Indian tradition. Gujral's work may not resemble the miniaturists' technique or subject matter, in that his drawing is not self reflective or personalised. However he

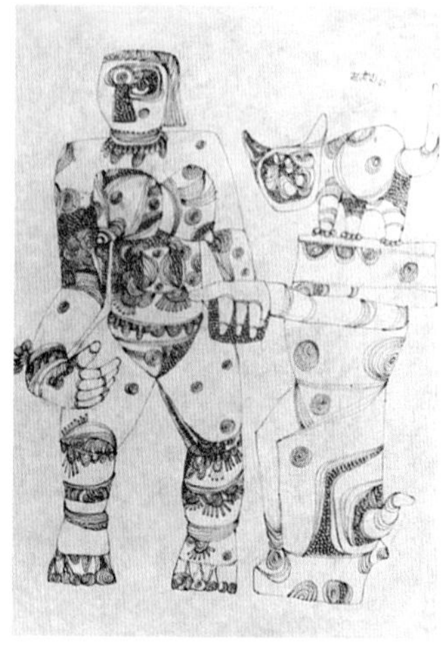

Untitled, 24" x 30", drawing

draws from subjects familiar in the domain of folk art, and works well within the parameters of a broad Indian tradition.

In the late 1990s, Gujral entered one of the most lyrical phases in his career. Figures of musicians and jugglers, figures evoked from the vast folk memory of northern India, succeeded his vigorous phase of burnt wood sculptures. The drawings that were executed parallel to this phase of painting had the same rhythm. These drawings were followed by the current drawings, in which proportions are simpler, and focus on the human figure to the virtual exclusion of other details. 'The body is more voluminous, and the head smaller, just as the writer or musician emphasises one or other part with almost photographic effect,' he asserts. The *bhava* or expressive quality on the face of the drawings of an earlier phase have made way for a more poetic proposition, in which the proportions and gestures of the figures accomodates nuances of humour – whimsical, even idiosyncratic. In a way, these drawings mark a sea change in Gujral's oeuvre.

The figure in his work, usually heroic in its aspirations, now admit the ordinary, even the mildly idiosyncratic in human nature. Gujral said in an interview: 'I have always been more interested in drawing, to let the hand flow. I believe that art is like a signature in its content, but the way you write . . . form is space and how it is drawn, and in this drawing is a recognition of what is happening within'.

What is happening within is perhaps a period of greater lucidity and simplification. Gujral has always been closely identified with a rugged, inventive use of texture. In the acrylic that he made for his paintings of the 1950s, the highly embossed surfaces of his ceramic murals, or the sinuous muscularity of his burnt wood sculptures, the texture has always been of primary importance. He opines: 'The material is the statement'. In the present drawings of musicians and acrobats, Gujral indulges in the light sensuous textures of rice paper. He also uses purely linear figures with a minimal shading, thus releasing the voluminous figures of musicians or the play between man and beast, that enact a rhythm to silent music. The overarching mood of a return to simplification reflects a more philosophic position. 'Art is archaeology, because like archaeology, it helps us understand ourselves'. There is an innocence here that belies the agitation of viscid paint or burnt wood, or sharp, metallic planes, suggesting perhaps that the artist has finally turned around the dark side of the pillar, into light.

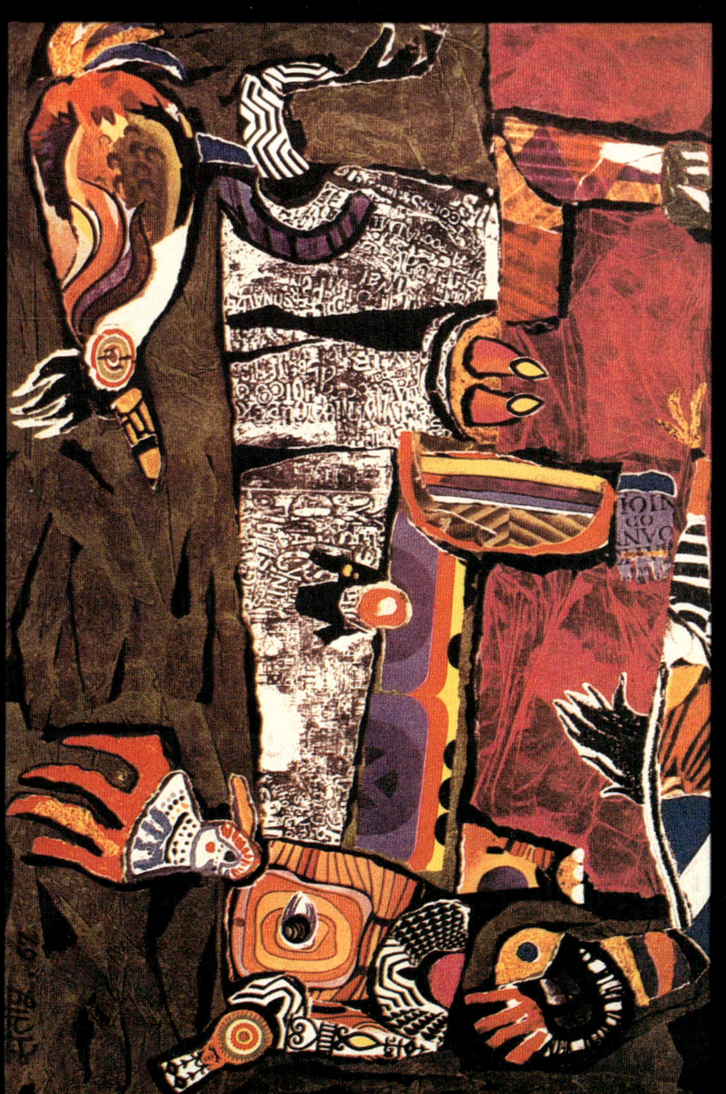

■ Playmates-2

22" x 30", *paper collage,* 1967

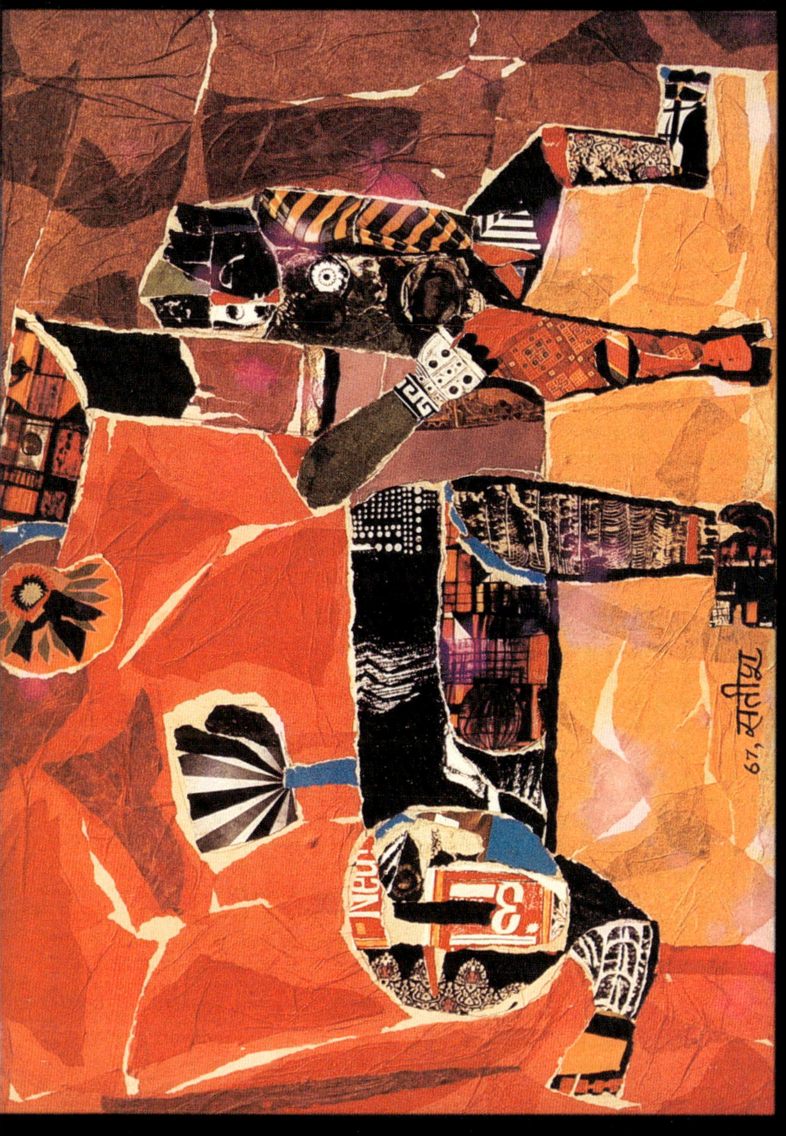

■ Playmates-4

*22" x 30", paper collage, 1968*

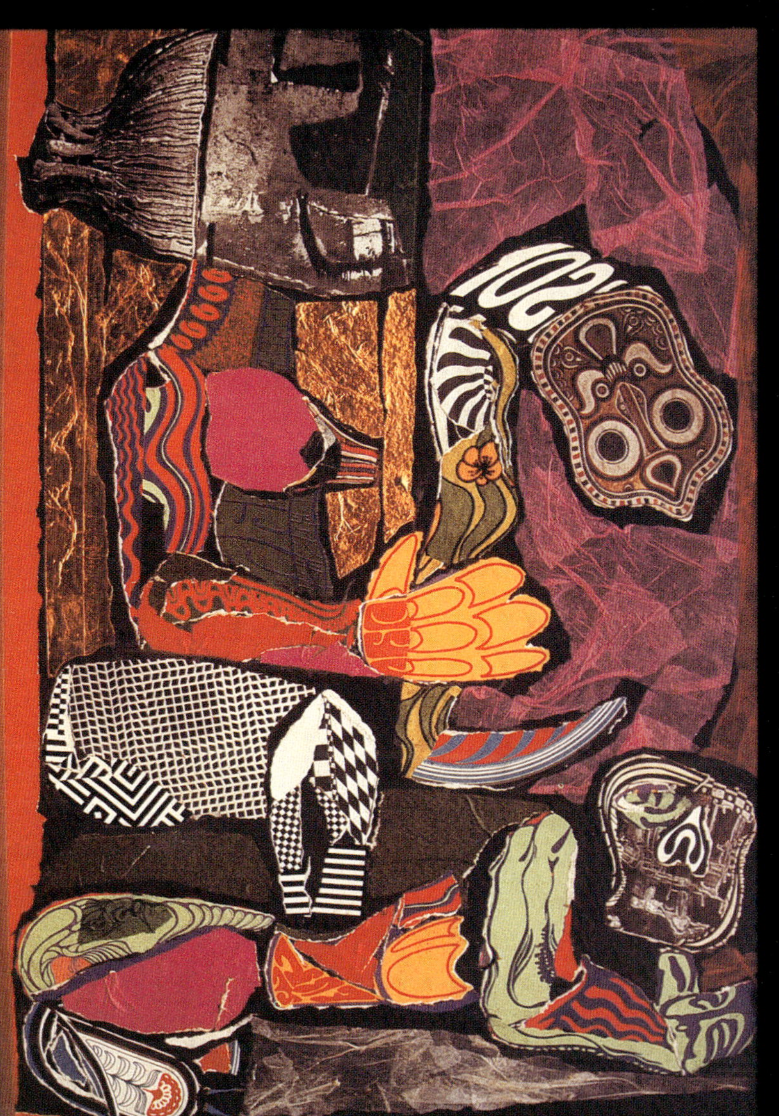

■ Durga

*20" x 30", paper collage, 1967*

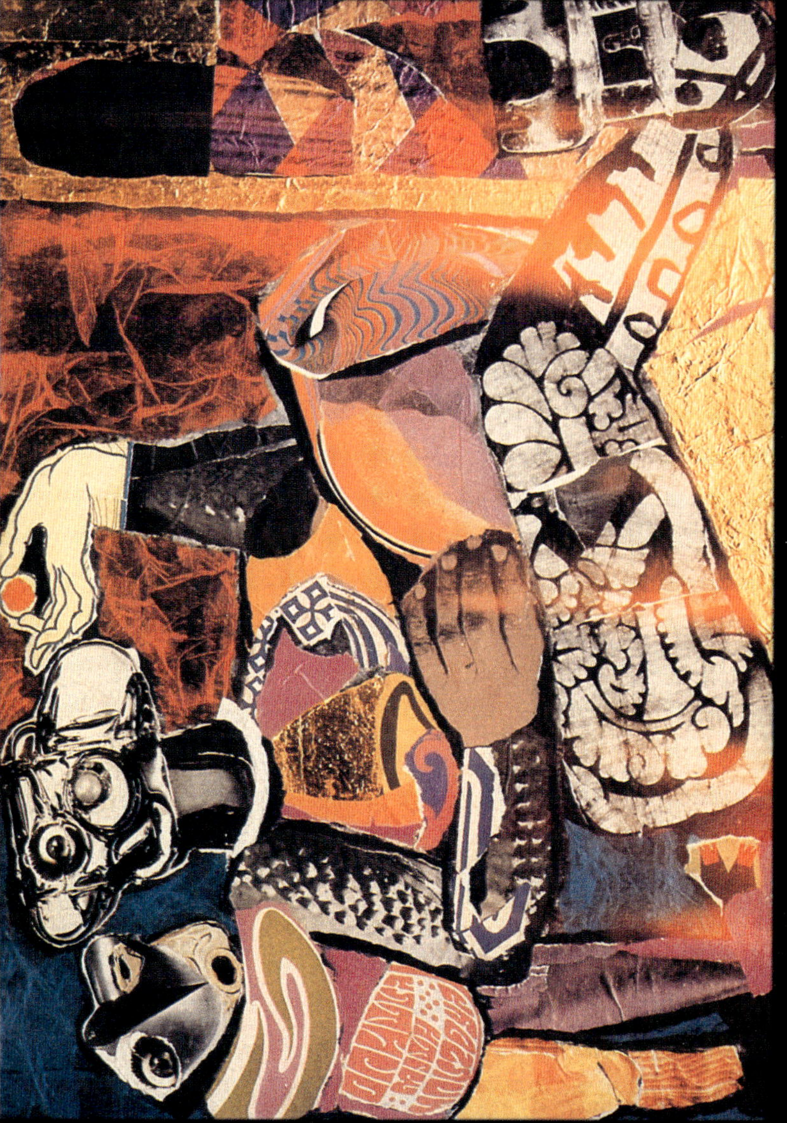

■ Resting

*22" x 30", paper collage, 1966*

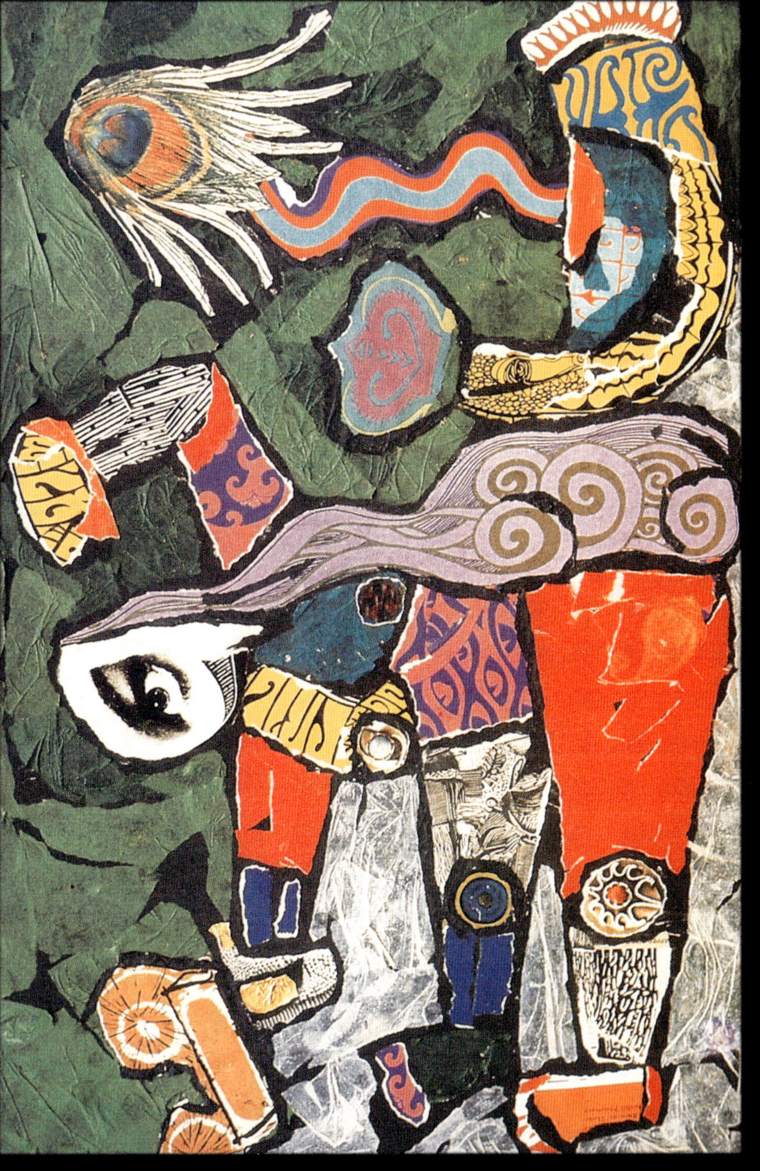

■ Fantasy

*22" x 30", paper collage, 1968*

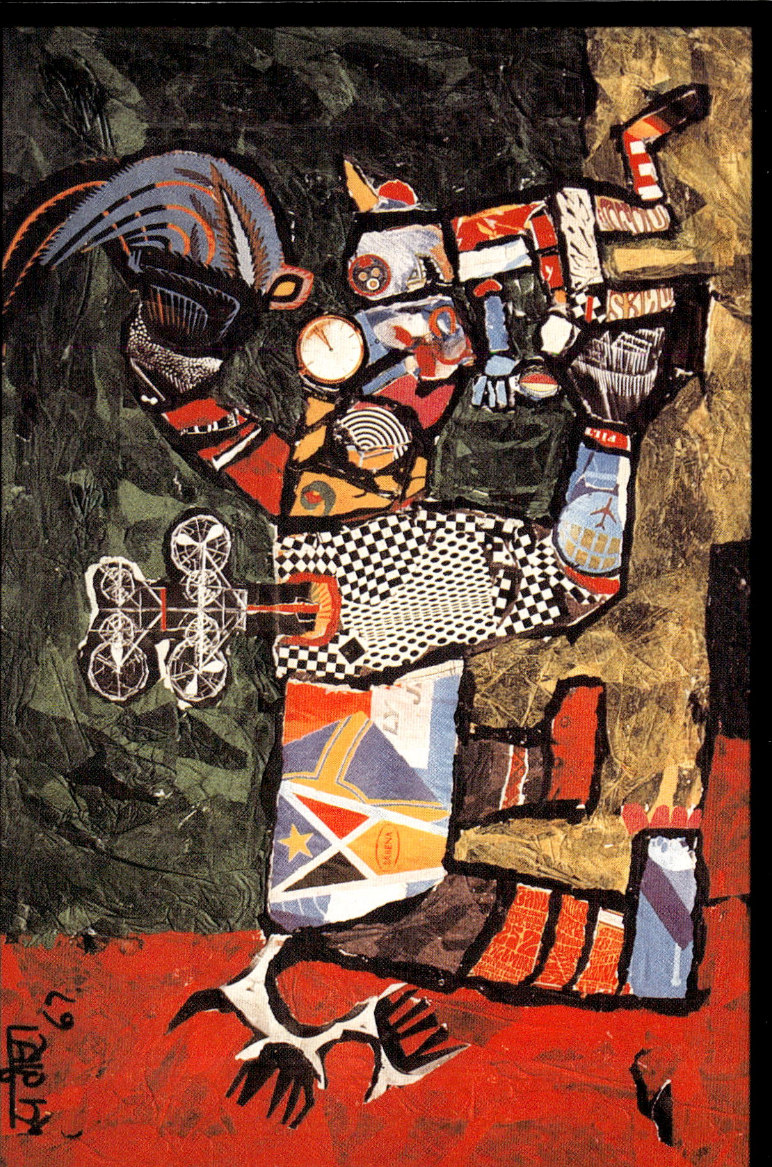

■ Mother & child

*22" x 30", paper collage, 1968*

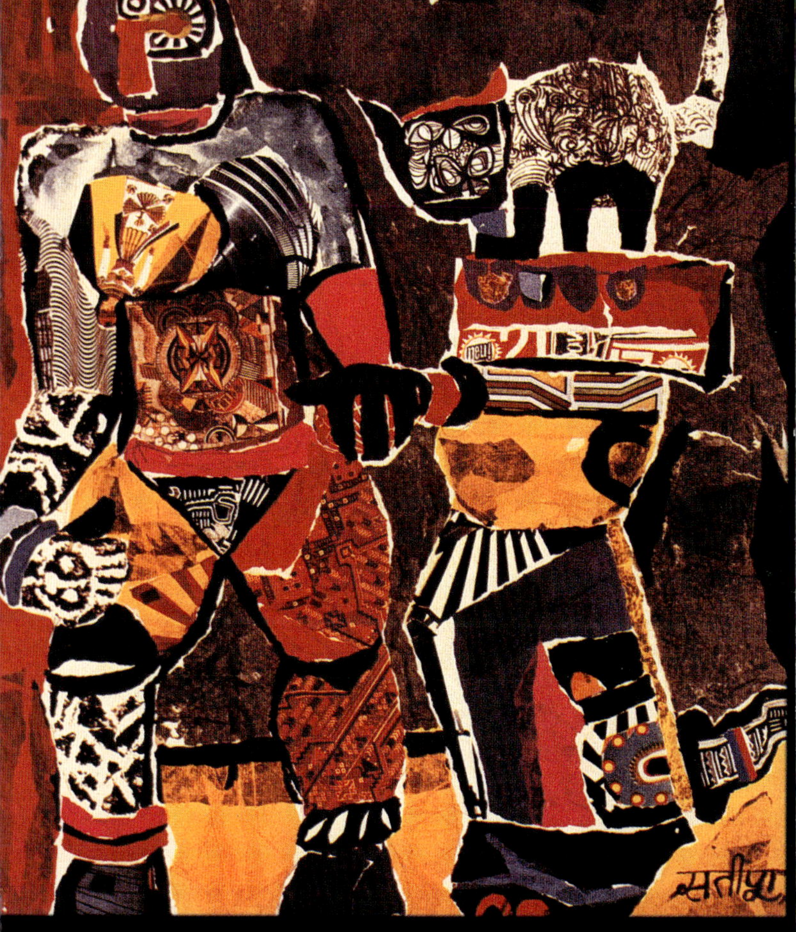

■ Playmates-I

*22" x 30", paper collage, 1968*

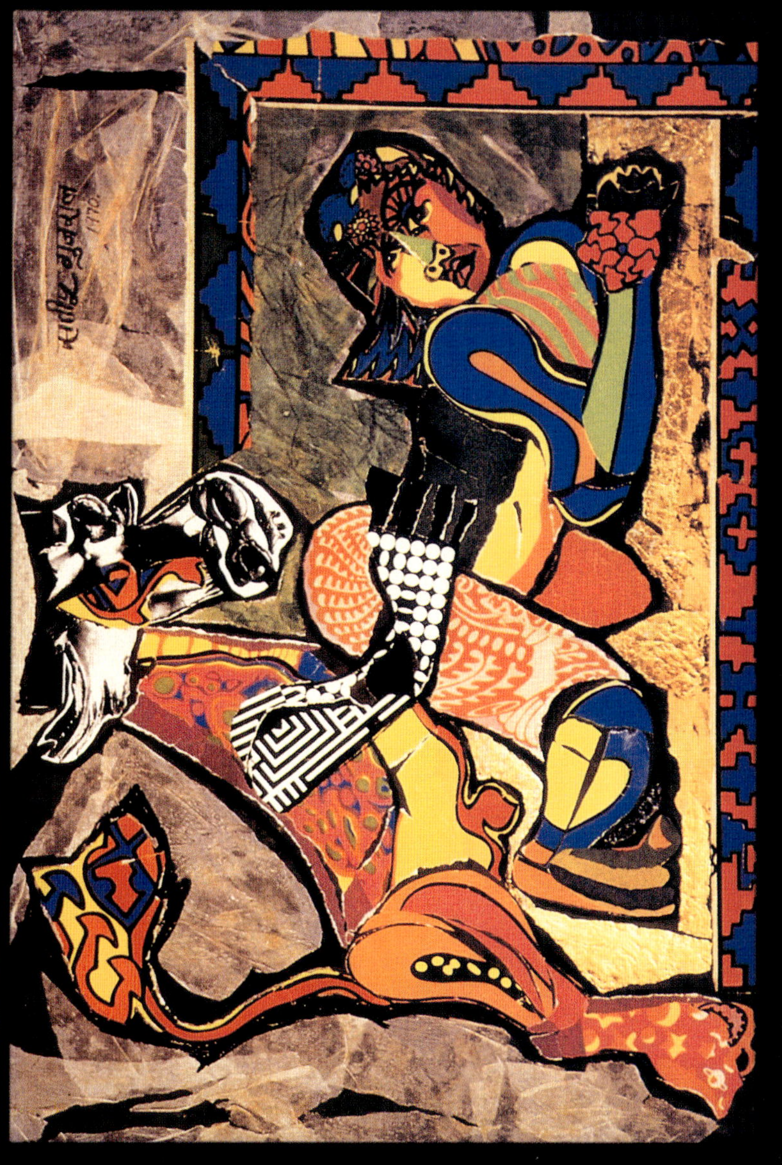

■ Playmates-3

*22" x 30", paper collage, 1967*

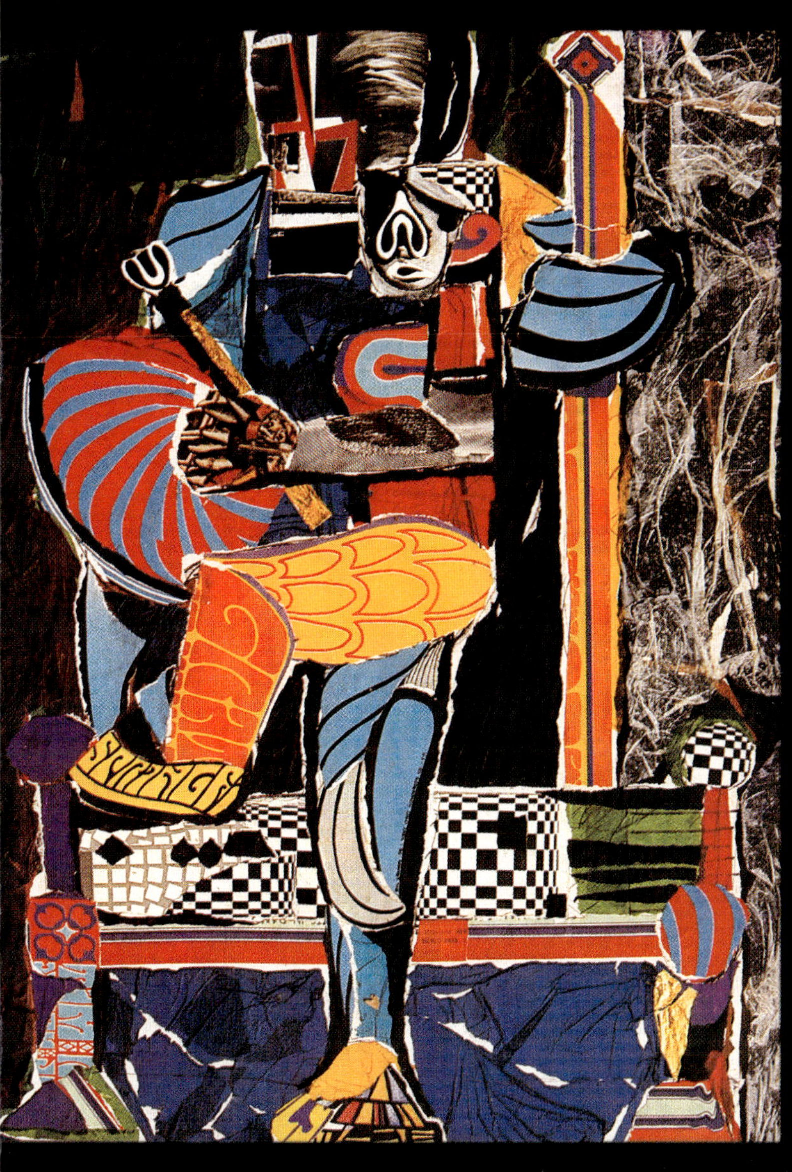

■ Lovers

*22" x 30", paper collage, 1965*

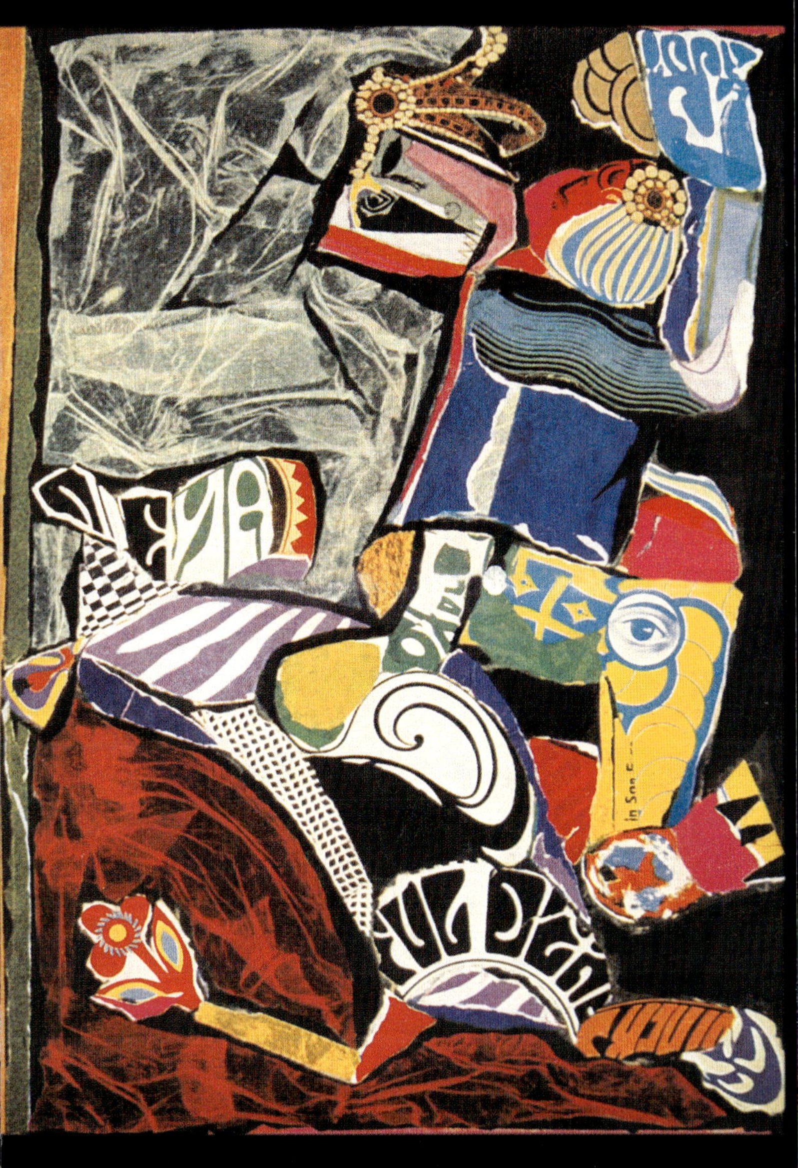

■ Beauty of beast

*22" x 30", paper collage, 1968*

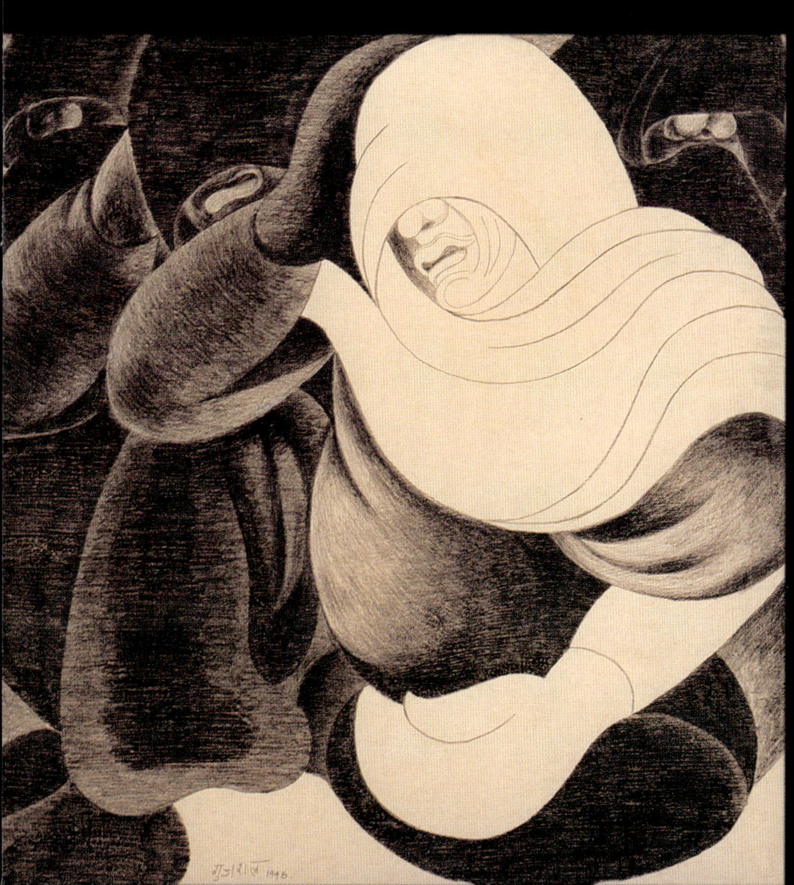

■ Mourning-en-man

*32" x 32", paper collage, 1952*

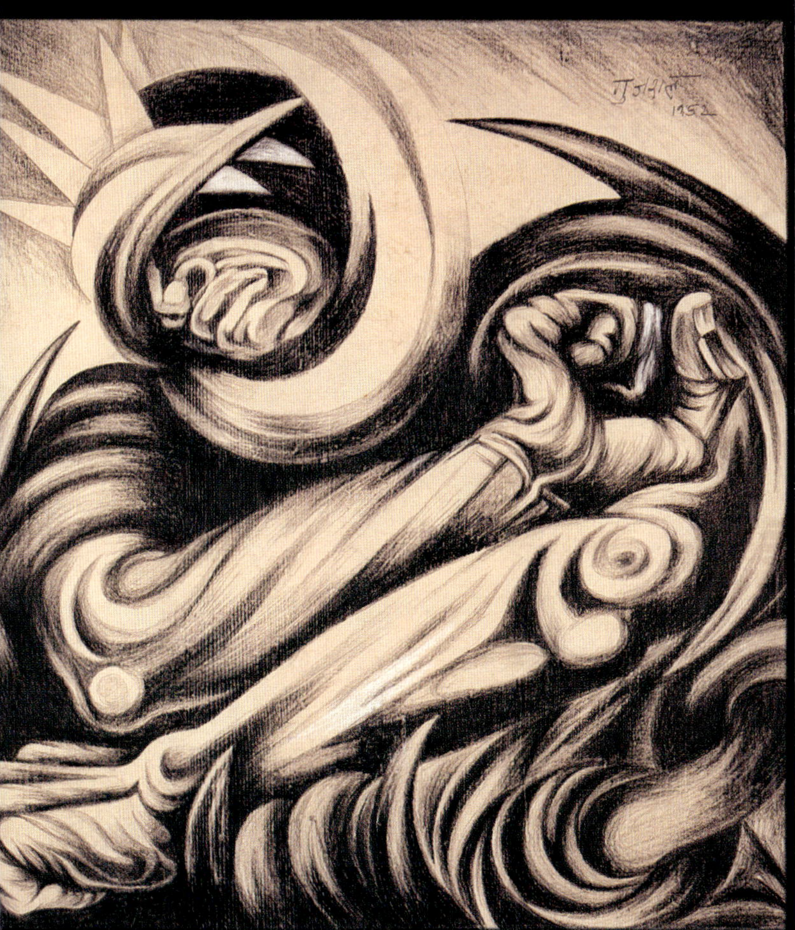
1952

■ Snare of memories

*24" x 32", paper collage, 1952*

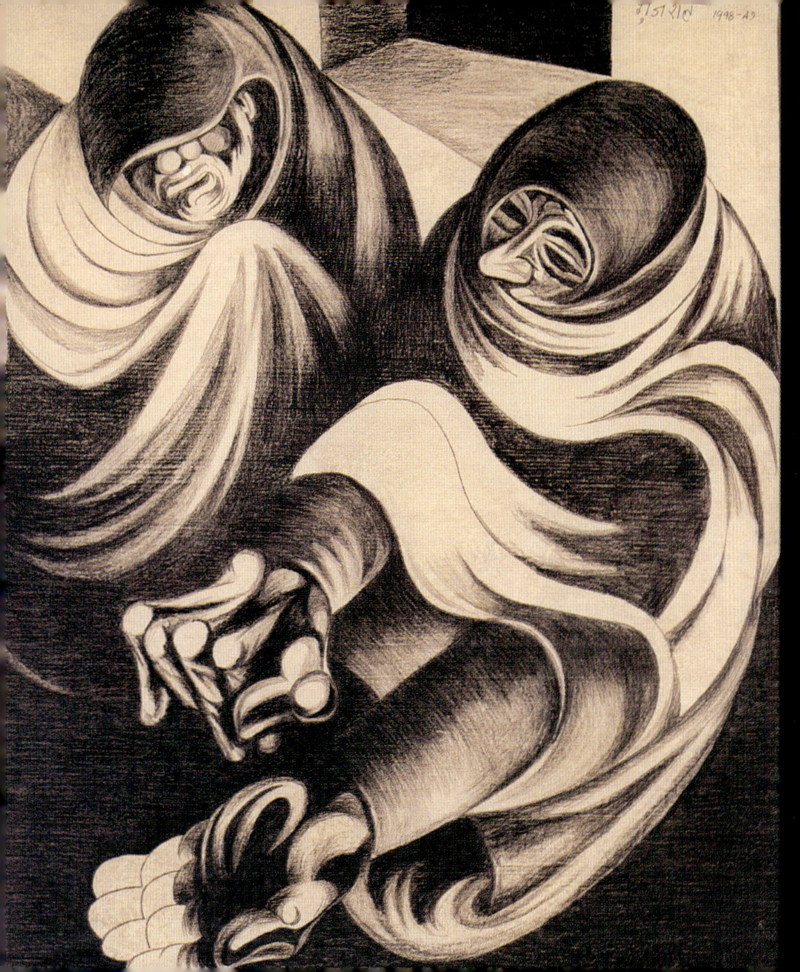

■ Days of glory

*24" x 32", paper collage, 1952*

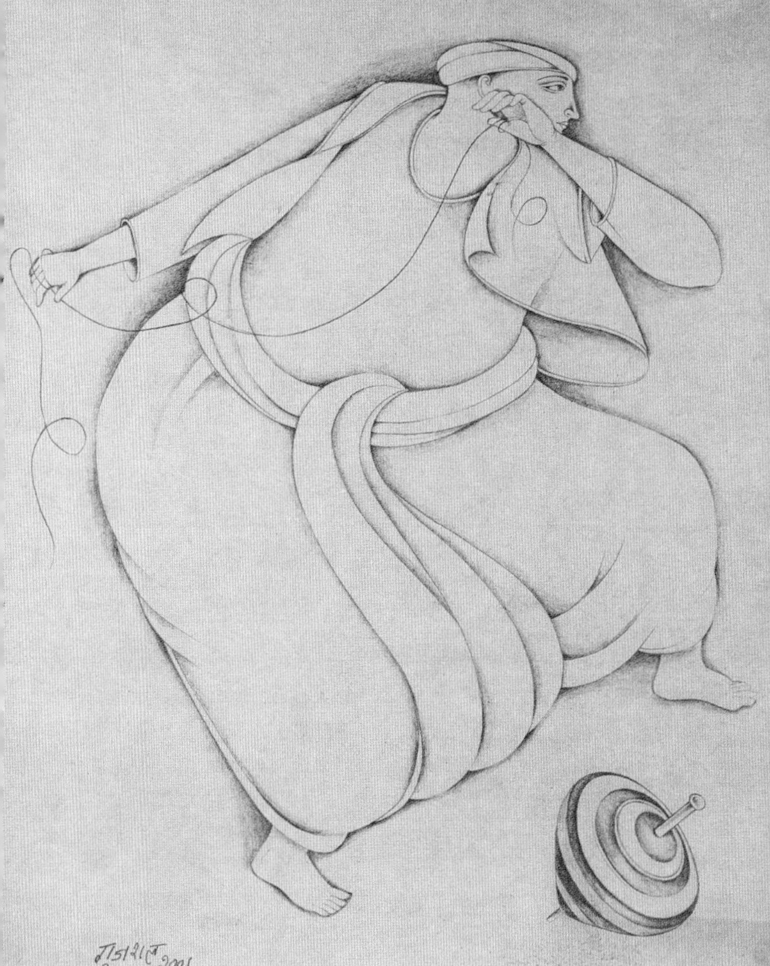
2001

■ Untitled

*20" x 29", drawing on rice paper, 2001*

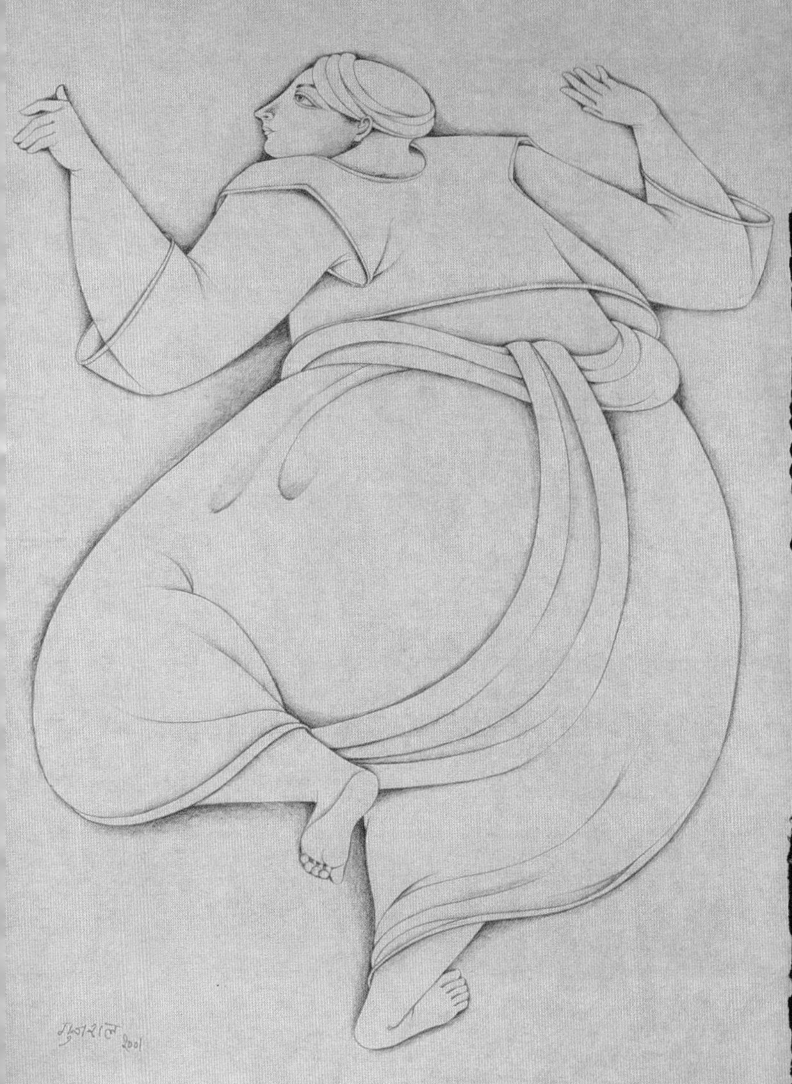
2001

■ Untitled

*20" x 29", drawing on rice paper, 2001*

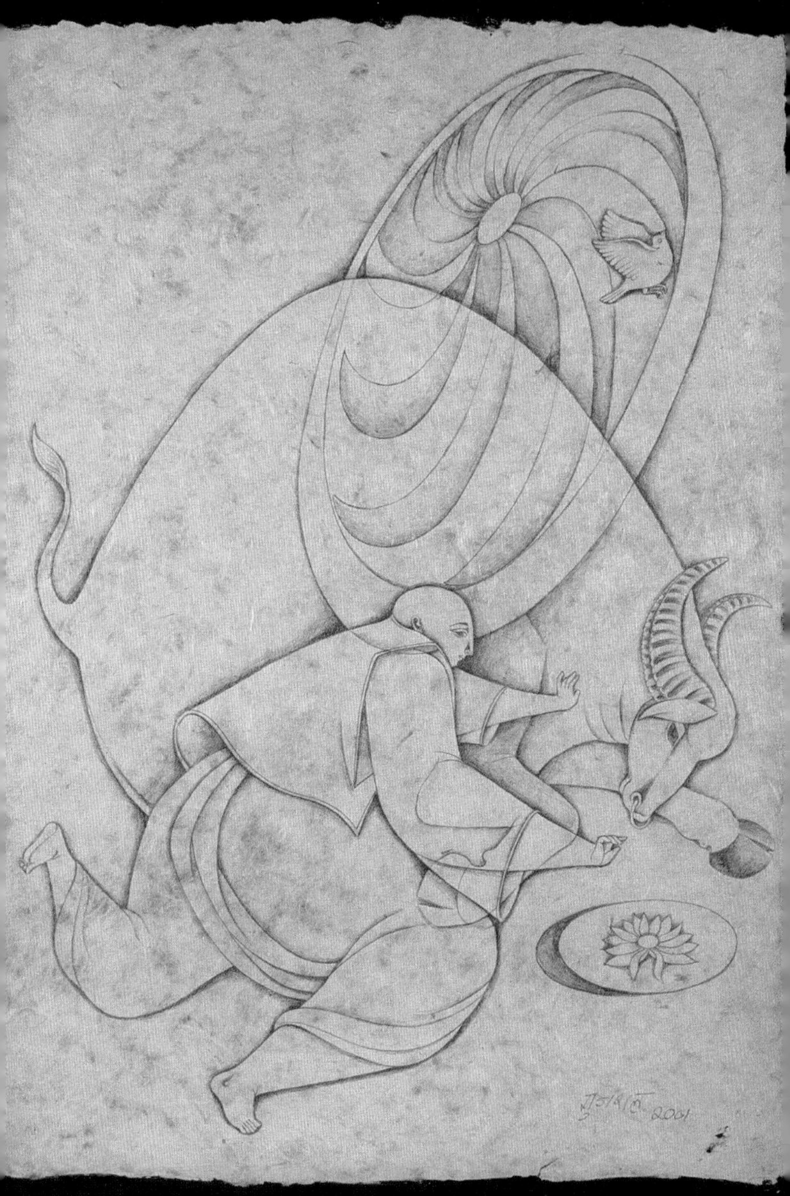

■ Untitled

*20" x 29", drawing on rice paper, 2001*

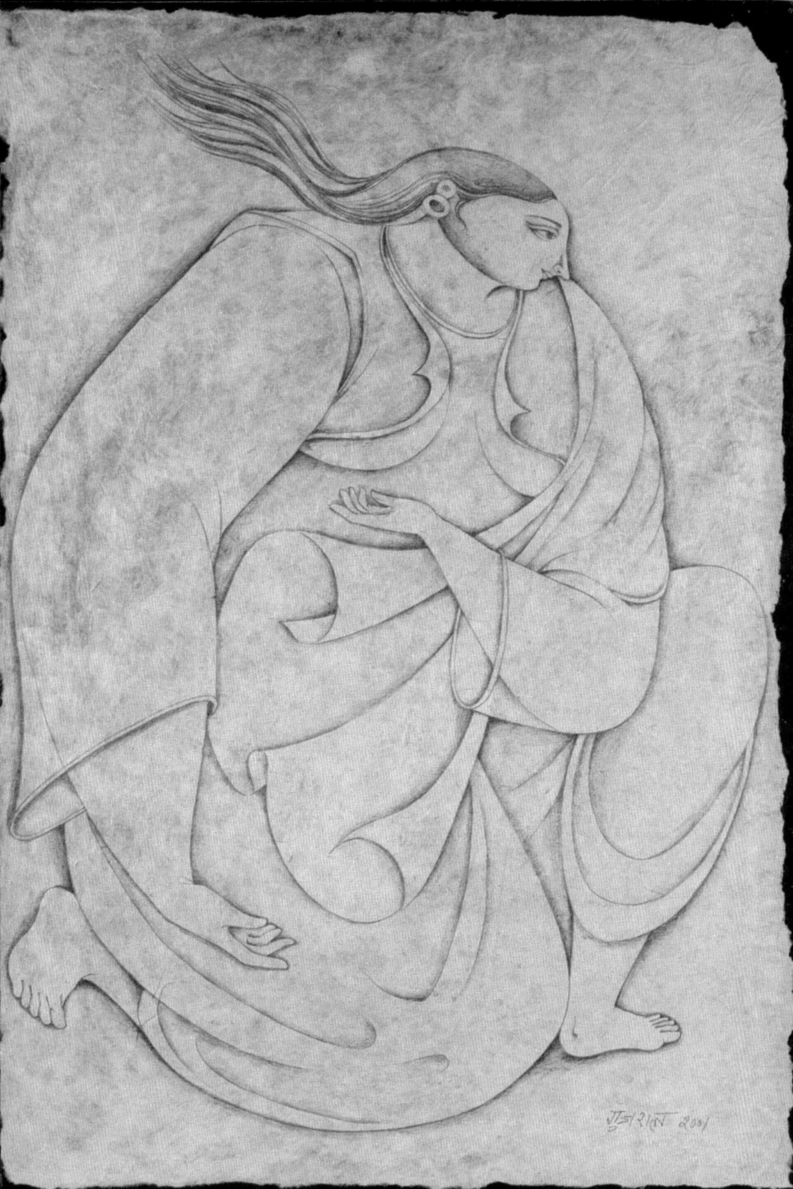

■ Untitled

*20" x 29", drawing on rice paper, 2001*

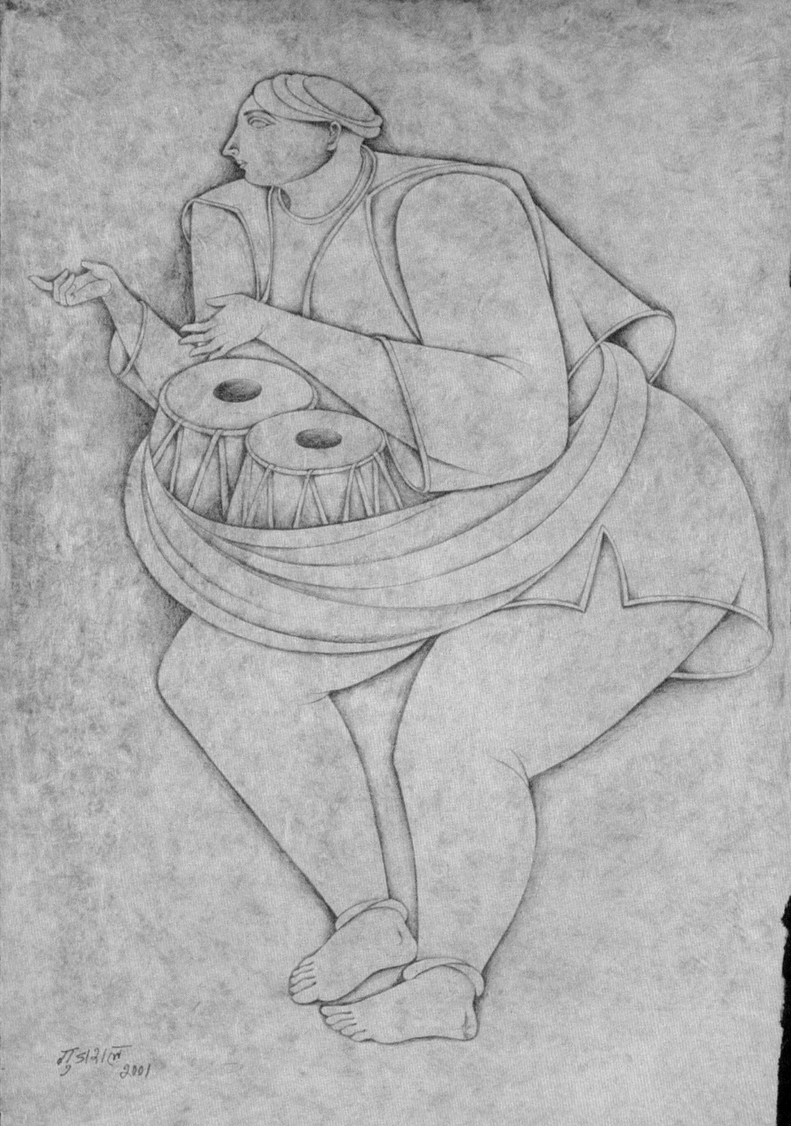
2001

■ Untitled

*20" x 29", drawing on rice paper, 2001*

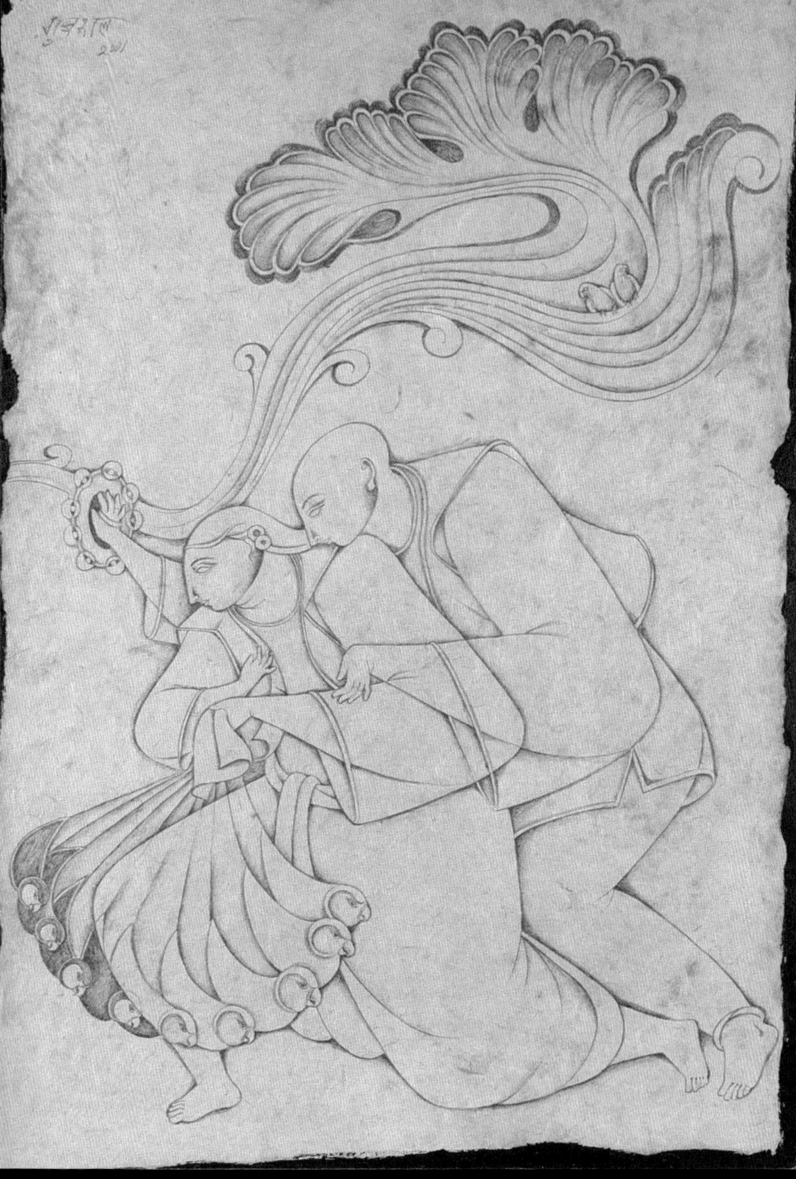

■ Untitled

*20" x 29", drawing on rice paper, 2001*

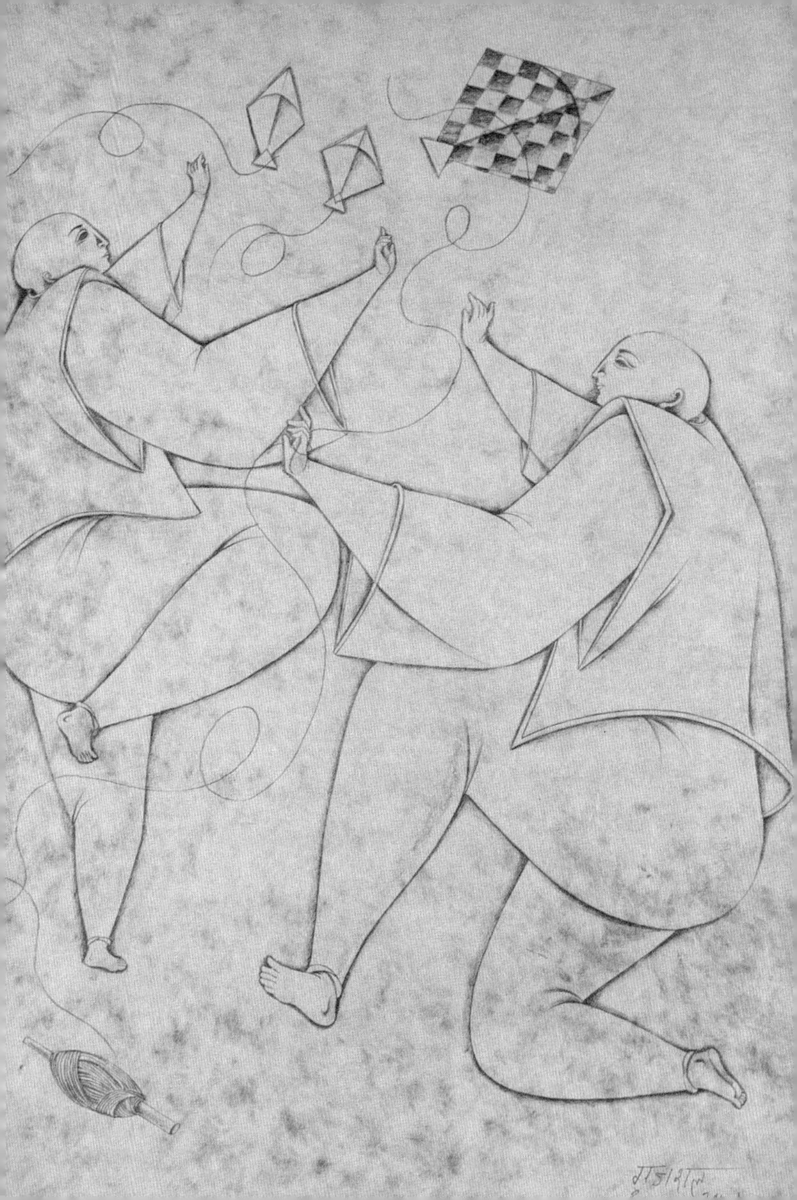

■ Untitled

*20″ x 29″, drawing on rice paper, 2001*

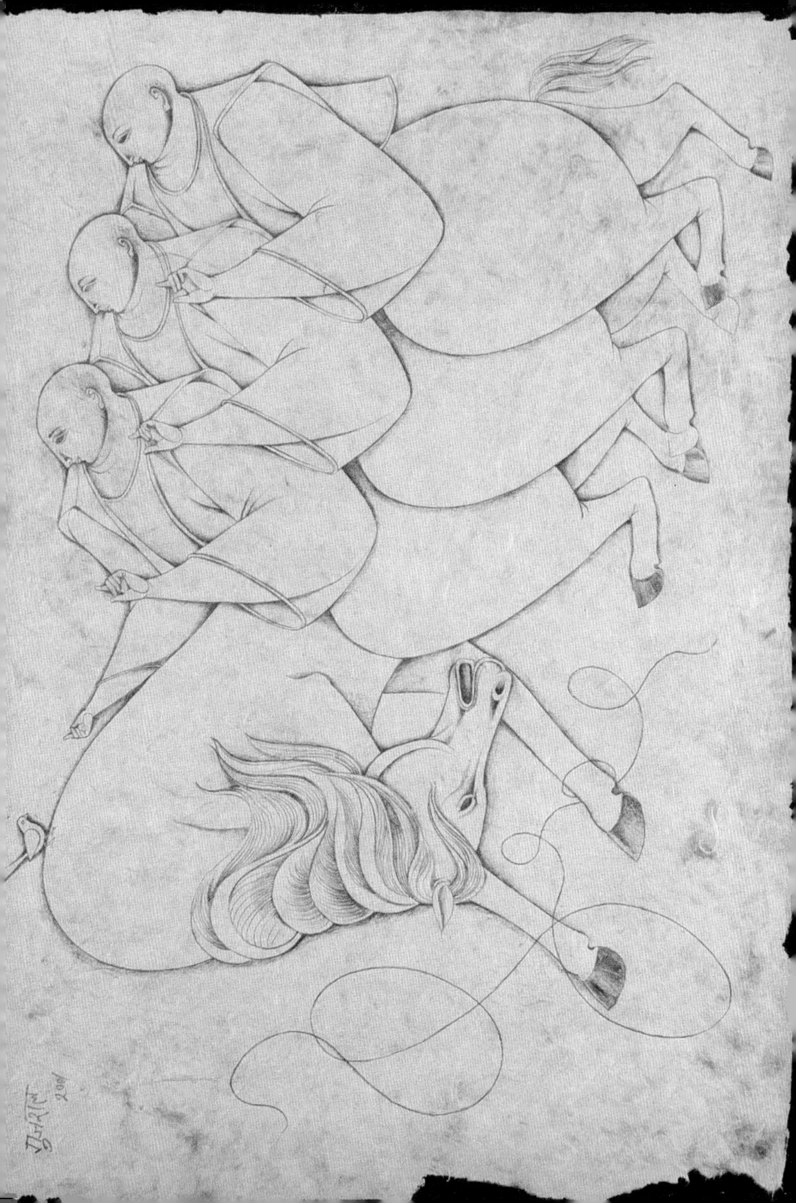

■ Untitled

*20" x 29", drawing on rice paper, 2001*

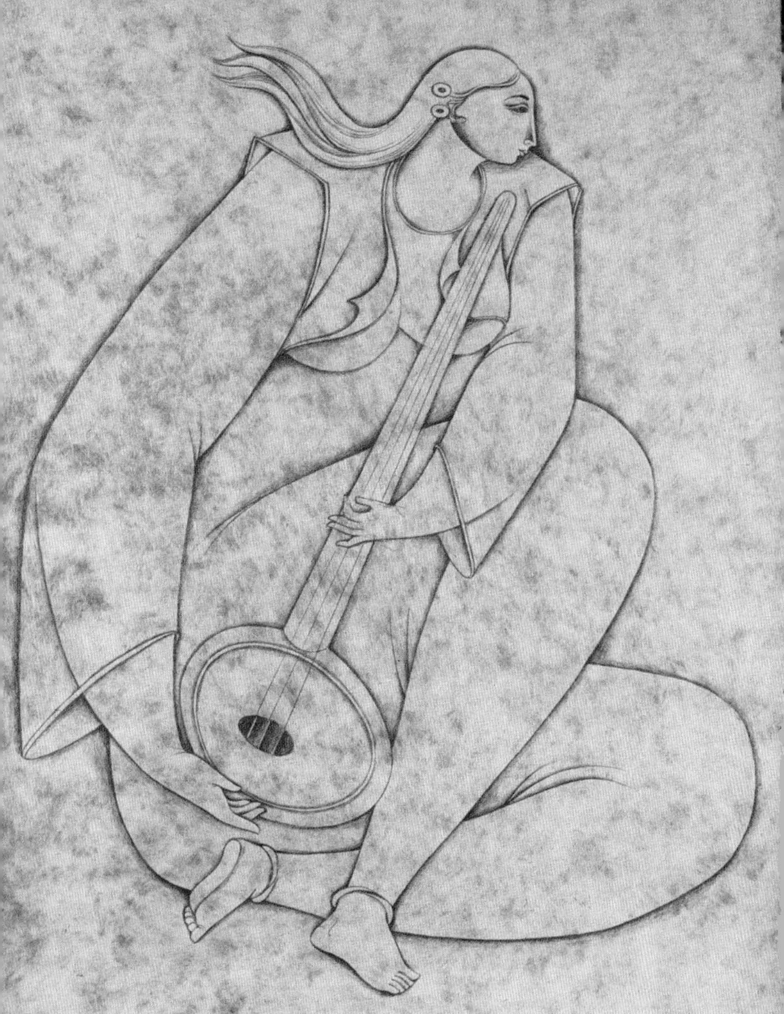
2001

■ Untitled

*20" x 29", drawing on rice paper, 2001*

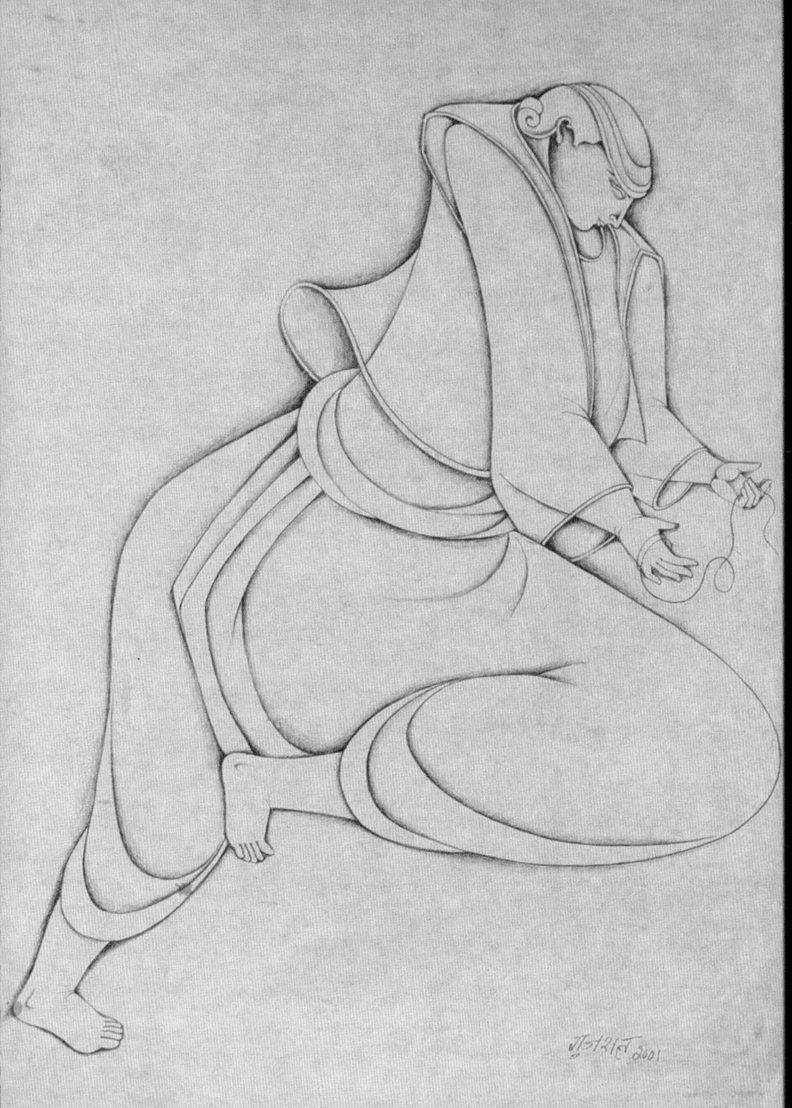
2001

■ Untitled

*20" x 29", drawing on rice paper, 2001*

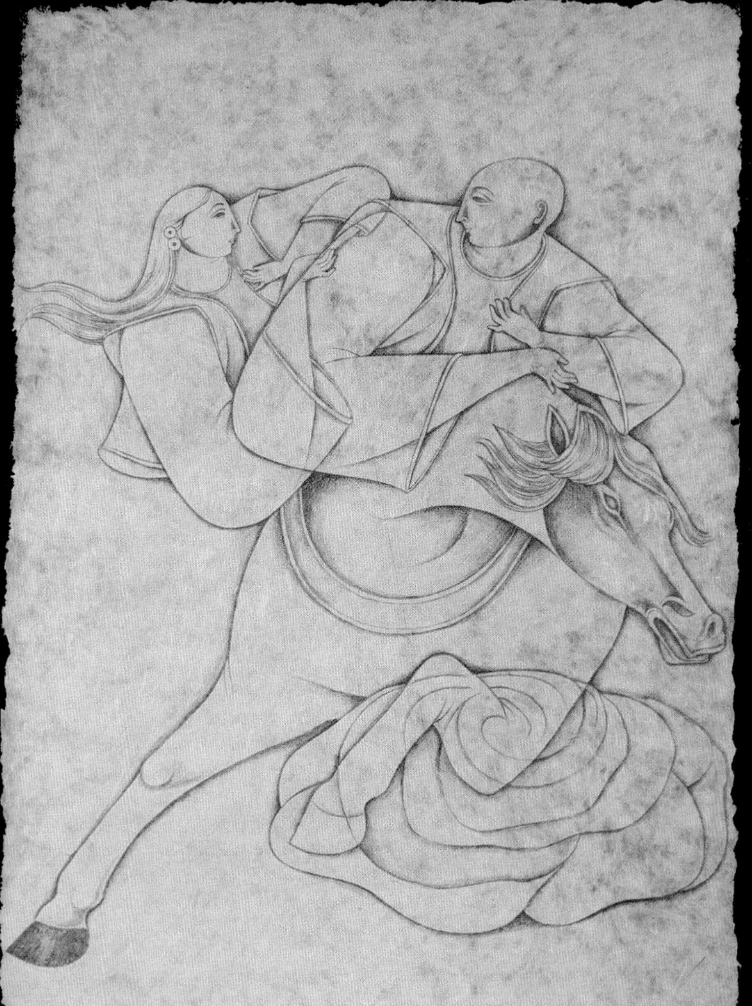
2001

■ Untitled

---

*20" x 29", drawing on rice paper, 2001*

■ *Front cover:* Temptation, 24" x 30", 1969

■ *Page 2:* Artist with his drawing

■ *Page 3*: Playmate, 24" x 30", paper collage

■ *Back cover:* Untitled, 20" x 30", drawing, 2001